The Lean Production Warehouse

By Alan R. Severance

Acknowledgments and Thanks

As always, I have many people to thank for helping to create this book, especially:

My *Beta* readers:

David Grubb and Darnall Daley, two experienced professionals who know a lot about people and Lean and how the two go best together.

Todd Pleasants, who understood that the warehouse function must not be separated from the rest of manufacturing and set about to create the new Lean warehouse.

Jon Sharp, the best Theory L Leader on the planet.

My Riverton colleagues, Dr. Miles Overholt and Kathy Crowley, for their active and ongoing help and support.

And of course my family, who support my writing efforts whole-heartedly. Thank you Diane, Julie, Jeff, Teresa, and Dick!

Contents

FORWARD

I have written this book for those who own, manage, or rely on a warehouse whose sole purpose is to support a manufacturing process. I do not concern myself with the huge cross-docking warehouses that currently supply countless outside customers with everything from aspirin to zip ties.

Those big, cross-docking warehouses may be Lean. Lean, after all is about reducing waste wherever it is found. They certainly are automated and impressive and if you've never been inside of one, I encourage you to take a tour. They have been 5 S-ed to a fare-thee-well, since nothing can be allowed to hinder the very rapid moving and sorting that embodies the essence of their existence. If a label is miss-aligned, a box will get kicked out of the queue and languish until one of the few real people in the building gets to relabel it and place it back into the system. This is really BAD! People who expect overnight delivery of their aspirin or zip ties get upset! Wouldn't you get upset if your copy of Liker's The Toyota Way wasn't on your door step the day after you ordered it?

Now, that's not to say that there's nothing of value in this book for those of you who are responsible for running these mega-warehouses. You will gain value from reading what I have to say about Lean and about people, because these principles will apply anywhere. All I'm saying is that I am not the least interested in these mega-warehouses. But I am deeply interested in your warehouse if its sole reason for existing is to supply a single customer – your company's manufacturing plant. Too many times, in my experience, the warehouse has been left behind or just plain left out of the Lean initiatives that manufacturers undertake and I think there are several reasons why.

For myself, I have to say my bias against those in warehouse positions got in my way. For many years, I simply overlooked warehouse improvements as something I could not control as a manufacturing manager. I viewed the fork lift drivers as under-motivated and overpaid, and their managers as prisoners of Inventory Control, unable to try anything new lest mistakes affect inventory accuracy. I never came across any warehouse employees who acted as if they were serving the people who were making money for the organization. No suggestion I made ever seemed to affect the response time or attitude applied to any request I or my supervisors made of them.

And while I seem to make light of inventory control, I will readily agree that accuracy in the warehouse makes a world of difference in how well a company can be run and how good customer service can be improved and maintained.

A final reason for lack of Lean warehouse efforts is that so few managers ever take the time to see how Lean can be installed, because most warehouse people usually work individually and not in teams with easily measured output. There isn't much literature available for you from Dr. Google, either.

Seeing a lack of books on Lean warehouses, I decided to write my own. Please come with me while I take a look at overcoming the barriers to Lean in the warehouse. I think you will find that with common sense and the right culture, you can integrate your Lean warehouse with your Lean manufacturing so that everyone will benefit from the ensuing synergy.

Chapter One:

Why You Want to Lead a Lean Warehouse

Lean began in manufacturing because there were so many obvious places to improve. We know that because we constantly measure production. OK, not really, but we measure output or invoicing dollars and compare the result to goals and budgets, last month and last year. Production gets measured every day, every week, and every month. It has so many ways to be measured that it's easy to do and easy to show the improvements. And in addition to any accounting measures of productivity, the improvements are easy to see: shorter production lines with fewer roller sections (all of these no-longer-needed sections were sent to the warehouse for storage, of course), delineated Kanbans which show reductions of W-I-P (all the excess inventory returned to the warehouse), decreases in cycle times (that require quicker response from the warehouse), space for additional production lines (which have to be supplied from the warehouse). Hooray for Manufacturing! They did it! They got LEAN!

Wow! Don't you wish you were the manufacturing manager instead of the warehouse manager? Well, take heart. Anybody can create a Lean production area. You are going to create a Lean Warehouse by becoming a true Lean leader, a Theory L Leader, someone who knows that Lean is best installed by finding more willing people to become leaders in the Lean initiative.

Think about what you need to succeed as a warehouse manager. You have to manage inventory in both a physical and financial way: you cannot bend it or break it when you put it away or retrieve it for production. You better not lose this stuff either! You have to have equipment that can do the jobs necessary and you have to be sure it is maintained and serviced. You have to have trained, knowledgeable, literate workers, people you can rely on to do the job right and come find you when they have questions. So how do you prepare to do this in a Lean way?

I think you must change your mindset from that of warehouse manager to that of supplier so you can partner with your customer to provide the best product and service possible. And while you start that, you need to take the same steps toward Lean that everyone else has. There are no short cuts! And you must be sure, as you begin, that everyone in your warehouse understands who their customer is, because for them it's not just "manufacturing," it is the person or the line or the shop that they deliver parts and products to.

Start by telling everyone what you want to do and why. Tell them what the new expectations are. Tell them why it is important to THEM as well as the company. Let them know that this is not a "management" idea or a fad. Make sure they understand that you are in this for the long haul and they must be also. Lean and 5 S are the way we do things around here starting now and never ending.

Now institute 5 S in the warehouse as the standard for keeping order. This is usually the easiest way to begin, since everyone understands the first principle of organization: A place for everything and everything in its place, just as your Mom always said. Explain what you want and be sure to tell everyone "why." Let them know that this is the first step toward Lean, and that the warehouse will be changing and training to become Lean by being organized, safe, and continuously looking for ways to improve.

While creating a 5 S warehouse, create teams wherever you can or treat your entire workforce as a team and teach the concepts of Ownership and Responsibility. Make sure that everyone has at least one assigned physical area which they will own, will be responsible for no matter what. It will always be clean and swept. Everything will be lined and labeled sufficiently that a new employee can walk into the area and immediately understand what belongs where. You want each employee to proclaim their proud ownership by the way they keep this area. In becoming a 5 S shop, they have created a safe, frustration-free work environment that is easy to access, and that is now free from excess material, unwanted items, and clutter.

After you see that they understand the concepts of 5 S, Customer, and Ownership, teach everyone Toyota's Seven Wastes. Be sure to add the Eighth Waste -

ignoring the skills and abilities of all who work in this warehouse. And be ready to answer some tough questions! Transportation is one of the Seven Wastes, but how can we reduce transportation? We are the warehouse and we have to get product to our customer in manufacturing. We have to transport it!

And indeed they must. But are there different ways to deliver items? Must everything be delivered by forklift? What about gravity-fed conveyors or overhead clips or hooks or buckets?

The warehouse associate at one small office furniture manufacturer I worked for asked if we could put in another door to the assembly area for large, bulky Gaylords (those sturdy skid-sized corrugated cartons) of chair frames. When the team on that chair line discussed it with their supervisor and the warehouse person, they decided that all they needed was a doorway big enough for two angled roller conveyors that would hold three Gaylords each, two on the warehouse side of the wall. We offered two frame finishes, black and polished chrome, and no longer had to worry about which frame was in queue. The warehouse material handler now had a visual signal (a Kanban!) that told him how long it would be before another Gaylord needed to be added to the rollers. Not only could he do it when it was convenient, he no longer had to respond to urgent calls from assembly telling him they were out of frames. While he still transported product, he did so without using as much of his time or having to stop something he was doing to respond. This worked very well so that when he came to me later with another idea, I let him jump on it immediately. He relocated some product within the warehouse and moved his frame boxes to locations across the aisle from the conveyers, providing even shorter "transport time."

You know, some "rules" about where things are stored in the warehouse were probably adopted a long time ago and may not still apply. If all of PART X items go "Here," do you have to live with that? One very good plant manager I know rearranged storage of all of his PART X's to be lined up in part number sequence for pulling, because his daily pick lists for pulling to production printed out in part number sequence. Pulling time for this product dropped dramatically, allowing the team who pulled PART X's some time each day to assist in Receiving or Shipping, reducing overtime in those areas.

Managing the Lean Warehouse means finding ways to continuously improve: your inventory storage and handling; inventory accuracy; providing accurate, timely delivery to your customers in manufacturing. I want you to manage a Lean warehouse, so that you provide the best chance for your firm to succeed.

One more caveat before I begin. I will use Lean terms throughout the book without further explanation, assuming you already know them or can look them up, but I will take a moment here to list brief definitions of some of the language used in this book.

Lean is the elimination of waste wherever it occurs in an organization. Toyota, the acknowledged leader in Lean manufacturing, listed as its Seven Wastes: Over Production, Over Processing, Excess Inventory, Transportation of parts and product, Movement of people, Waiting, and Defects or Rework. US management usually adds an Eighth Waste, ignoring or overlooking the skills and experience of the people who actually do the work.

These Wastes are often described as Non-Value Added, usually defined as steps or activities that a customer would not willingly pay for if they knew you were doing them.

5 S refers to the Japanese system for organizing a safe, productive work station or work cell, in which you: Sort items that don't belong there; Set in Place any Work-In-Process (WIP) and tools and supplies that remain; Shine this area by keeping it clear of trash and clutter and by making sure tools and equipment are kept in perfect condition; Standardize these practices, making them routine and automatic; and Sustain this effort and appearance – forever.

Kanbans are part-specific, quantity-specific locations for parts and production output. A Kanban is typically a two-bin system so that when a bin is empty, it can be removed for replenishment while the second bin of parts is immediately available to keep production moving.

Theory L is my concept of Lean leadership that says a Lean initiative in any organization can only be sustained when the effort is people-centered, where support is cascaded through every level in the organization, and where focus is on finding and developing more Lean leaders throughout the organization. Please see my previous book, <u>The Human Side of Lean Enterprise</u> for more on this topic.

Chapter Two:

Start with 5 S

5 S is the go-to kick-off for most of us who teach or practice Lean. It is a very non-threatening way to introduce new behaviors for all employees, especially team play and problem solving. The concept is simple. You want to have a safe, clean, well-organized warehouse so you can serve your customer with good product in a timely manner while correctly accounting for the inventory.

If you haven't already done so, assign everyone to an area that they must be responsible for and then convince them that they own this part of the warehouse. Tell them that this means they are responsible for everything that happens to product assigned to their area and for the housekeeping in this area. They must OWN this area. If inventory is off, they own it. If parts are damaged, they own them. If 5 S breaks down, they own it. You will hold each of them, not someone else, responsible for anything that goes wrong. And you will give them due credit for everything that goes right!

As with other hard concepts, you have to insist on ownership in these terms, reminding people often what it means in this warehouse. Most everyone will get this. Any that don't should not be working in an area this important.

What do they do with the stuff they own? They must deliver it to their customer when it's required, promptly and in good shape.

So what's not already 5S about a warehouse? After all, a warehouse is just a bunch of racks for skids of storage, with probably a staging area off the Receiving Dock for stuff waiting to be put away, maybe a parts cage, maybe a bench to kit parts, or floor space for bulk or bulky items.

Well, it doesn't hurt to review even the best of warehouses against the 5 S's.

SORT: Is everything in the warehouse properly identified, labeled, and located? Are there items in the warehouse that do not belong? How about the fans used by production in the hotter months? What have you done with them and other like items? What about machines, machine parts, conveyor sections, ends and crossbeams for additional racks? Are items such as these taking up valuable warehouse space? In fact, are they taking up prime space on floor locations, near the door to production or next to the receiving department? Do they block access to items needed frequently? Who do they belong to? Who OWNS them?

Probably not you if you're the warehouse manager! They were dumped on you because manufacturing didn't have enough space or a permanent spot to put some of these things. So if you have to store them for your customer, do so, but put them out of your way and advise your customer of their locations and how much lead time you will need later to retrieve them.

Do you use your red tape and red tags to identify items you want taken care of? Better yet, do you call the owner of a particular area or process when you see a 5 S violation? Do they know you want it dealt with immediately?

SET IN PLACE: What about scrapped and rejected material? Do you have any in your warehouse? If it has to be there, is there a designated spot, properly identified, and available to decision makers? Who ARE the decision makers? Do they know they have stuff to review? Who tells them it's here? Who is responsible for storing and pulling these items? Who OWNS them?

Do you use your racks as tools rather than just storage bins? Do operators know to put little-used items up high and frequently pulled items lower or even on floor locations? Transportation is a Waste in Lean environments, though it is often necessary activity for items that cannot be stored at point-of-use locations, so you must be vigilant in reducing the time it takes to pull the popular items, saving your material handlers time.

SHINE: Is the warehouse free of trash? More importantly, is the warehouse set up to easily remove packaging and other trash as part of the operator's normal duties? Is excess packaging normally removed from those skids or locations when parts are pulled? Is all banding removed when skids or Gaylords are taken to production? Are all excess packaging, stretch wrap, corners, and cleats taken back to the warehouse by the material handler?

Better yet, is it possible to <u>safely</u> remove any of the packaging before parts leave your Receiving dock? This shortens the time it takes to pull these parts when they're needed, and usually shortens the trip to the recycle bins.

Are all rows, racks, bins, skids and parts correctly labeled? Does tape or paint identify floor locations? Is black-and-yellow tape used to show where industrial trucks are not permitted to go? Mixing people and trucks is always problematic, so do your best to clearly label pedestrian walkways.

Are safety and warning signs at all appropriate locations, correctly sized and colored, clearly seen, and in multiple languages where necessary?

Is all equipment safe, clean, and well-maintained? Hoses and belts wiped down every day? All safety equipment and seat belts are good? Do you routinely touch up the paint on your industrial trucks? Do you use a daily check-list as well as an hours log for all your mobile equipment? Has everyone who uses these devices been thoroughly, correctly trained?

STANDARDIZE: Anyone can make a warehouse Shine. The real question is: Can you make it Shine all the time? Are the practices described above in place and understood by everyone? Is there a formal training guideline for new employees, and in all appropriate languages? Does everyone know where cleaning tools and supplies are located? Does everyone know where to find 5 S supplies: tape, labels, bins?

When you can institutionalize the Shine of 5 S, you will be able to say you have Standardized. This comes with thorough training, constant reminders of expectations, constant follow-up on your part, and holding the owners of the processes and area accountable. Never let poor 5 S discipline go unnoticed.

SUSTAIN: Is 5S now part of the culture of the warehouse? Has the behavior of all employees changed to acknowledge that this is an integral part of their job, not a clean-up or project or idle time make-work? When you change the expectations and demand accountability from every employee, you achieve the sustainability that only behavior change can bring.

All the above is very well in theory. Execution requires your dedication and relentless effort. You need to be able to plan to deal with the constant addition of new parts, the reluctance of Inventory Control to deal with obsolescent items, any seasonal demand for parts or space, and all reluctance to deal with scrap or rejected items.

What can you really do with all the stuff you end up with? Let's look at some practical ideas. And I'll start with the biggest headache for most warehouses: empty skids. You end up with all of the skids coming in. Of course you do, you're receiving product on skids. Some product is removed from the skids before you put it away. Some is stored on the skid it came in on because you can put it safely into the racks without extra handling. Some of this product is taken off the skids before delivery to the manufacturing customer. And of course some is delivered to manufacturing still on the skid, and your customer will return the empty skid to you when all of the product has been used. Or at least make you come get it.

No matter what path skids take in your building, they all come back to you unless your company is able to reuse them to ship outgoing product. That is the absolute best solution possible but not always an available one. But don't just pile empties behind the building! I hate seeing these stacks because they are more than just an eyesore or fire hazard. They are a clear signal that the company is not Lean and no one has taken ownership of the problem.

As the warehouse manager, it is your problem. Period. No one else will own it. No one else will remove the skids. So decide what you are going to do and make your plan. You CAN get rid of them in a Lean manner.

I have seen warehouse managers use all of the following ideas.

Send them back to your vendors on their trucks. Trade them to your pallet supplier for the kind your Shipping Department needs. Sell them to local pallet makers who will resell them or take them apart to reuse the cut wood. Ask your recycler to take them, and ask what they will pay you for them or ask if they can at least remove them without charge to you. Burn them in the incinerator you use to heat your building. And I will bet you have even more ideas from your own experience.

The point is, any idea that doesn't require treating excess skids as trash is a Lean way of disposing of them.

While I'm on the subject of recycling, let me remind you that talking with your cardboard or scrap metal recycler may show you some other ways to be both Lean and Green. I am sure you are already recycling these two items, because you can get paid for doing so. So talk to them about every other item you throw out. They may be willing to take the plastic banding or stretch wrap material you generate when unpacking in-bound freight. You might even get really lucky and discover that one of the country's very few Styrofoam recyclers is in your area. Again, if they can't pay you for an item but will haul it for free, you still save the cost of trash removal. Ask your Accounting Department what one load of trash costs! Not only will you be surprised by the amount, but you can quickly quantify the savings you and your warehouse are making to the company's bottom line! And the results add to your firm's Green story that the Marketing Department will use with customers.

To keep our expectations and instructions clear, let's go now to the subject of language, an increasingly important factor in warehouse management.

Chapter Three:

Language is Important!

We need a common language in order to be understood when we communicate. Common sense, yes? It is when we think about communication carefully. And I submit that it is more important today than it has ever been. Many of you struggle with multicultural, multilingual workforces. This is the first communications hurdle to overcome.

The second is the introduction of new concepts, which often means using words in a context not previously thought of.

The third hurdle is to clearly define even the common words and phrases we use every day if there is a possibility they may be misunderstood.

And lastly, we may want to use specific words or phrases to signal a change in attitude or behavior that we wish to make in our organizations.

Lean leaders understand this because they begin their efforts with new meanings for existing words such as Lean and Waste, and because they introduce new words – including Japanese words! – to their teams.

Regarding the first communications hurdle, I will have to let you find your own resolution of your workforce language problems, except to say that the more bilingual team leaders you can find, the better off you will be. And every important sign you post or instruction you print must be in as many languages as you need to keep your people safe, secure, and informed. Even if your company standard is English, definitions, examples, and explanations must be given in a second language to ensure complete understanding.

My own language skills are minimal, limited to English and the little bit of French I can recall from high school. I'm forced to rely on bilingual associates to help me relay Lean concepts to a workforce, so I have adopted the philosophy that Key Words will be English (or Japanese!) even where the explanations must be in another language. When taught this way, everyone in the organization understands "Waste" or "Lean" or "5 S" in common usage. This is my approach to the second hurdle and is easily augmented with signage, handouts, and other tools. I have long believed that if a message was important enough to post, it was important enough to be in all of the appropriate languages. I started with Safety signs early in my career, ensuring that all my employees understood the expectations regarding Safety. It was a natural for me to continue the practice with 5 S and Lean initiatives.

So what is *Lean*? How will you describe it to your people as you teach them the new way of thinking about how they approach their jobs? If you haven't created your own internal definition of Lean and what it entails, you will be stumbling and fumbling as you attempt to get others to listen. People want to follow someone who knows what he or she is talking about! Make sure you know before you attempt to lead others.

Another strong suggestion I have is to use the English and Japanese words now accepted in the literature. A young supervisor once asked me why he shouldn't call Kanban squares by another name if it made sense to his people. And if his people were the only work team in the company, he could probably do anything he wanted and it would not detract from his Lean efforts. But he could not use a different name in a company where "Kanban" was already used by all the other departments and work teams. Use of a different word would only work to confound communication with others. We will have enough to do to establish a Theory L culture without reinventing the names and labels already in common usage.

And while I'm on the subject, let me throw out another common word for you to think about: *communication*. I use the following definition for this word. Communication is the PROCESS of transferring a thought or idea in the mind of one person into the mind of another with the SAME EXACT MEANING. It is a process, something you have to actually think about while doing it. You have to consider your message, the best way to deliver it, and how you will ensure that it was received and understood. You have to be good at organizing your thoughts, good at delivering them, and even better at listening. If you do not understand the concept of Active Listening, find a book, video, or teacher and learn it at once. It not only makes you a better communicator, it saves you an incredible amount of time and angst!

Communication is an active, on-going process. Never assume you have communicated without checking for understanding!

Other troublesome words are the ones we think that everyone already knows!

Customer comes quickly to mind. Who is your customer? Is it the Big Box Store that buys the output of your factory? Or the Internet consumer that orders one or more of your products? To succeed in providing any product or service, you have to know who your customer is. And if you run a warehouse for a manufacturing firm, or work anywhere in that warehouse, you have to understand that the production line that takes the parts you are pulling is your customer.

Many years ago I was the manufacturing manager of a large office furniture company which also had a separate division that sold textiles to other manufacturers. Because the Textile Division had all the technical knowledge and owned all the inventory, my operation was effectively just another customer. In fact, I thought that I was the Division's biggest and most important customer. The Division head and I had the same boss. Our manufacturing operation was the largest single user of textiles from their warehouse, which was located adjacent to the manufacturing warehouse.

So when my boss asked why a particular order had not yet shipped, I discovered that my internal supplier had not sent me the requested fabric. Well, this will be easy to solve! I walked to the Textile Division to speak to my counterpart there, where I'm told that the fabric in question was in short supply and what was on hand was promised to "a customer!" Well, what was I? So I asked the director to tell me who the division's biggest customer was, and when I was immediately given the name of a competing furniture company, I melted down. Silly me! As a Sales Division, the Textiles people were paid bonuses on their outside sales, but not for "shipments" across our campus to my upholstery area! I was fuming, but now I understood that the word customer might not mean what I thought it meant!

Clearly, I never forgot this lesson.

Responsibility and *ownership* are other over-used, misunderstood words and must be clarified for your people. You want them to accept responsibility for their part of the process, their part of the warehouse, and the condition of their equipment. You want them to believe that they own these things, think of them as their own property and treat them accordingly. If they merely pencil-whip the lift truck's daily service log, they are not feeling the responsibility. What do you see them do? What do you insist that they do? Do you hold them accountable for the state of their equipment? Do they carefully look over their lift truck each day, checking for problems, oil leaks, broken lights. Do they keep it clean, free from clutter, lubed and checked, fueled up without your constant reminder? Do they go the extra mile, ask for paint to touch up the scratches on their equipment? What about the area of the warehouse that they are responsible for?

Responsibility is for outcomes, not items checked on a page. Good or bad, they are responsible for the outcome of everything they undertake. You won't see the best of Lean efforts until every one of your people accepts ownership of the equipment, product, and processes they are responsible for.

My last concern about language is the understanding that words matter, that the specific labels we give something make those things real for us.

What do you call your warehouse operators? It does make a difference. "Fork lift drivers" drive fork lifts. All day. They leave items of packaging and trash in the warehouse aisles because they can't reach them without getting off the truck. I've seen them drive to break and lunch, even to the time clock at the end of their shift. Remember, I mentioned in my Introduction that I began my manufacturing career with a dislike for the way I saw fork lift operators behave!

Successful warehouse managers call their people "material handlers" because they put away or deliver products all day. They may use industrial trucks. They may use pallet jacks. They may have to walk an item to their customer or push a rolling rack of parts. They do some of each of these things every day as they do their jobs, handling the material that they have accepted responsibility for. For these reasons, we need to call a material handler a material handler, not a forklift operator.

Chapter Four:

How the Heck Do You Measure Warehouse Activity?

Measurement is necessary for anyone to do a job properly. Without meaningful metrics, we can't know if we are doing our jobs well or poorly, or if we're improving or falling behind. Most of us want to know how well we are doing, especially when we think we are doing a good job. Many types of measures are used in warehousing, and I don't care much for most of them. Who cares how many times a particular skid is "touched" or a specific warehouse location is "visited?" These depend on customer demand and become meaningless for measuring activity. If a location is visited multiple times a day because manufacturing efforts require it that day, that is simply a fact. Now this information may show an opportunity for process improvement or problem solving, but it is not necessarily an activity that is measurable in a meaningful way.

I prefer using the same method for the warehouse that I teach for production: Units per Full Time Equivalent Employee, or Units/FTE. This measure allows direct comparisons and shows trends regardless of the number of hours expended, people used, or the number of days per week or month.

Teams learn that adding people to get more product is not always the Lean way to proceed. Teams learn to measure the amount of output per day or per week as a factor of the number of people applied. If U/FTE (Units produced or delivered, divided by the number of Full Time Equivalent employees) drops when more people or overtime hours are applied to get more output, everyone can immediately see what this costs and why the company cannot continue to solve problems this way.

Using the FTE number, instead of actual staffing numbers, allows direct comparisons of several different operating conditions: half days, overtime, extra people, or part time employees. The process is to convert all applied hours - the hours worked by the number of people - divided by 8 for a day or shift or by 40 for a week's efforts. Tracking the weekly number will show trends and improvements. When the team leader reviews the numbers each week, he or she has the perfect opportunity to discuss the successes made and the impediments discovered, not just as explanations of the numbers, but as opportunities for instruction or problem solving. A note of caution here: All means all hours. There are no deductions for meetings, breaks, or any paid time, though you will deduct unpaid lunch times.

This measure is most accurate when the units in question are roughly the same. It would be meaningless to compare U/FTE of delivery of an aircraft engine to the assembly line to the U/FTE of delivery of the attachment bolts for that same aircraft!

Why will the employees trust this number? They will calculate it! One of the first assignments to be made or, better, volunteers called for, is to have several team members trained in calculating the number and reporting it. The team owns the number; it is the result of their demonstrated effort. And the team must calculate the number and be ready to discuss the results.

The results and any discussion are for understanding and education. Period. They are <u>never</u> a club, even when results show a decline. The team will learn the factors that impact their performance. They will learn how to use the numbers to decide how many people are needed for a given output to be maintained or to determine how many more items can be produced in a day or a week when demand makes increased output necessary. You and your supervisors have the same advantage when asked or tasked by senior management to determine capacity levels. All of you will have real data to base decisions on, instead of trying to do a rough-cut capacity plan on the fly.

This gives real data to the team for the team problem solving efforts.

It is also easy to calculate and easy to track. These are both important because you want your employees or teams of employees to calculate their own results daily, weekly, and monthly, and to see the results over time. You can provide a convenient form with the formula spelled out, so all they have to do is apply the numbers and calculate: two people worked for six hours and delivered 225 part X's to their customer on the production line. Twelve hours of labor divided by eight hours in your scheduled work day equals one and a half Full Time Equivalent Employees. Divide into 225 units delivered today and today's measure is 150 Units/FTE. Simple and understandable. And directly comparable to yesterday even though you had two people on this activity for ten hours each because of the demand from your customer. Yesterday's Fulltime Equivalent is two and a half people, twenty hours worked by two people in total. If yesterday they delivered 400 part X's to the line, the Units/FTE was 160.

Now you have two numbers to compare. You can begin tracking your month to see if there is any trend. You begin to see your demonstrated capacity. If production needs 150 part X's, you only need one person for eight hours to supply them; if they need 500, you may need three people with some overtime for each of them.

Now, to get on to the fun part. Your warehouse team devises a new way to deliver part X. The Units/FTE after the change will tell you how much they have gained in productivity by making this change.

How else can you measure your warehouse? As with any human endeavor, I like to manage Quality. For your operators, quality may mean looking at things differently than in Production. Your delivery of product to your manufacturing customer is a service, so you will want to measure the quality of the service you provide, and one way to track this is to create a log for every time that parts or supplies are delivered wrong. The evaluation of these issues provide your teams with opportunities to improve their quality.

So what do you track, specifically? Most people immediately think of handling damage, delivery of a part that is unusable because it was damaged in transit. And of course it is part of your quality measure, one you must attack every time with additional training; your customer cannot use bad product.

And there are other things that can be measured that impact your customer's ability to do his job. Every time an incorrect part or quantity is delivered, make a note; this is also a direct measure of the quality of the job your people are doing. Again, you have opportunities to correct mistakes, and more importantly, prevent recurrence. The time you spend solving these problems will improve your quality measure AND your productivity! After all, only good parts can go into your Units/FTE calculation.

Inventory Accuracy is another important measure, and not just for the Accounting Department. Your customer relies on you and your people providing accurate counts of product being put away and of product being taken to the line. The wrong quantity of the right part still slows your customer's flow unnecessarily. Shortages will cause Waiting time to increase. Overages require time and proper handling to return to you. Either way, your customer has been forced to slow down and your own people have to go into Rework mode. Rework is not just an assembly issue! It happens in the warehouse and must be dealt with. It hurts your Units/FTE measure, but most importantly, it can lead to damage to the parts in question. It is because of the added risk to product of this unnecessary extra handling that one of my supervisors once declared that Rework is the biggest cause of Rework!

What else can be measured? Your floor and rack space. Thorough 5S practices and better control of processes will provide you with opportunities to consolidate space, relocate items, put away returned items without staging them first, and rationalize your inventory by consolidating all PART A's in a single location. This last example can be significant if PART A is a large item.

Proper Inventory Control practice says accurate count and location are sufficient for managing a warehouse. Part A can have multiple locations and it doesn't matter where they are physically located as long as quantity and location are accurate in the system. Common sense says that in addition to accuracy, physical location can reduce transportation costs and time and will facilitate actual First In, First Out practice. Ever dealt with FISH instead of FIFO? First In, Still Here inventory is much more likely to happen if one random location is so far physically removed from normal activity areas that everyone knows what a pain in the neck it is to go there.

All of these measures must be understood and used by your team members. It is by measuring their own impact on the warehouse activities that they understand their contribution to the effort. As a Theory L Leader, you are looking for others in your organization who will also step up and lead, and this is how you begin. Pay attention to those who understand the Lean efforts and are trying their best to adopt them. These are the people who will be your next generation of Lean leaders.

Chapter Five:

Attacking the Eight Wastes

I want to remind you that Lean is the elimination of Waste everywhere it occurs in your company, not just in Production, so that as you review the list, understand that all do apply to your warehouse and all can be reduced, if not eliminated. Even Over Production applies to the warehouse, and I'll get to that shortly, but I want to address the 800 pound gorilla first: Transportation.

Transporting product from any location in your building to any other location is a Waste, a Non-Value-Added activity. Period. That's what The Book says. Yet this is your job! Your people have to bring good parts from the warehouse to fill the Kanbans on the production lines. So all day long they are engaged in wasteful activity, right?

I don't see it that way. I don't even want to go to the Non-Value-Added-but Necessary category because I believe that if an activity is necessary, it must somehow be adding value to the overall process. Instead, since Transportation is your primary purpose, it provides most of your opportunities to become Lean. In fact, we have already discussed some ways to reduce transportation, such as storing parts at the point of use, storing fast moving parts closer to the doors into the production area, and even using roller conveyors to let product present itself to the point of use. In each of these cases, Transportation has been reduced by the people who are responsible for it. They have identified the issues that this Waste presented and devised workable solutions – some of them very creative solutions.

And there are other ways, small and large, to contribute to Transportation reduction. Warehouse input on Kanban size is an example, and something that has to be problem-solved in conjunction with your customer. They are your customer but not your king and you must apply common sense to every Kanban decision. Production will want smaller or larger quantities or containers than you might want. That's OK, but determine the final Kanban size together to get the best possible result.

Over Production is one Waste not usually associated with warehousing. After all, your people don't produce anything, don't transform a raw material into a subassembly or finished good. Well, there are many ways to over produce and I'm sure you'll think of examples as you read my two favorite ones. Pulling more product than is required for your pick list or a Kanban is Over Production. So is staging product to be delivered later. Staging may mean a shorter delivery time to the production department, but it requires extra handling and floor space. If you have agreed with your customer on Kanban size and replenishment times, there is no need for staging.

What these examples are telling you is that there is a problem to solve. Time to go ask the Five Whys and discover the root cause of the action or request!

Over Processing is another Waste you will suffer from and it takes many forms, some not always recognizable. Do your people pre-inspect items to be pulled for use? The process is to receive good parts, put away good parts and pull and deliver good parts. Where does it say "Inspect"?

Unless your people are scratching, dropping, or damaging the product they are pulling, they are delivering good parts. Your process says so. Why the need to second guess? Again, you are dealing with a symptom of something and not the cause. Time to meet with Receiving, QA, and maybe your vendor to determine what quality level is acceptable. Do what you have to do – move the responsibility back to the owner of this problem without making your customer suffer.

The Waste of Movement is usually associated with excess moving from station to station on a production line. It is the movement of the people themselves that is the waste – they cannot produce while they are moving to another workstation, or worse, back to a previous station. But you're in the transportation business, so your material handlers have to be moving, right? Of course, but moving back to the warehouse empty after delivering parts is a waste. Taking an empty lift truck to Production to retrieve empty Kanban containers is a waste. So is taking an empty pallet jack to retrieve the daily collection of trash from Production.

Production lines aren't the only entities that can benefit from studying the Value Stream. Create a spaghetti chart of each of your material handler's daily movements with them and have them tell you why each trip, in either direction, is required. Once you both understand exactly what the current effort entails, look for ways to shorten or combine trips, eliminate dead-head trips, and reduce the total number of trips. Most obvious is to make every delivery trip a retrieval trip, whether you bring back empty Kanban containers, trash and recycle, or broken or damaged parts. Check to see if near-by production lines need servicing. Get really creative and meet with several adjacent lines to reconfigure Kanban size and replenishment that minimizes delivery trips without interrupting production flow or creating excess W-I-P.

Waiting is always listed as a biggie, typically because in Production it is a huge detriment to one-piece flow and the production processes that accomplish that. How does the Waste of Waiting impact the warehouse and what can you do about it?

Are your material handlers waiting because Production has no empty Kanbans? This is certainly the best reason to wait – unless it's a sign that some Kanban sizes or delivery cycles need to be adjusted. Kanbans aren't etched in stone, and will require review periodically, from your perspective as well as Production's. Are they waiting because Receiving is flooded with in-bound parts today? Go help unload!

And do your operators know what to do with any enforced Waiting time? Are they routinely sweeping, replacing worn or damaged labels and signage, doing the tasks that Sustain 5 S? Are your Continuous Improvement Teams meeting to share information or problem solve? Can you cycle-count important, fast-moving, or problematic parts? Can you get a jump on your Annual Physical Inventory?

That's a BIG time waster, right? An Annual Physical Inventory all by itself meets the definition of most of the Eight Wastes! The good news is that every Lean improvement you undertake will make the Annual Inventory smoother, shorter, and more accurate. Your 5 S efforts alone will help you here. When all parts are correctly stored and properly labelled, you will have fewer miscounts, fewer misidentified parts, less shrinkage – fewer bumps! The actual count is easier and more accurate, and is much more likely to agree with the Inventory Control system. You cannot eliminate this time-waster on your own; your accountants will dictate that. But you can greatly reduce the negative impact on your warehouse operations. Who knows? If your operations become so tight that the cost of taking the inventory is significantly more than the cost of shrinkage, you may see the end of the Annual Physical Headache.

I use Rework, not Defects, to describe the next Waste because Rework can occur with a perfectly good part or product. If you deliver too many items, those parts have to be retrieved and put away. Rework. And Rework is my favorite Waste! Every item of rework is an opportunity to improve a process and this is how your team will continue to get Lean.

Why did a perfectly good "PART A" get returned to stock? It was not needed by the production line.

Why? It was in excess of their demand.

Why was it pulled?

See where this leads you? You can find out if the root cause was a mistake in the Bill of Material, a misprint on the picking list or a miscount by the operator pulling it. Once you know the cause, you can correct it. Without doing this detective work and problem solving, you won't prevent recurrence, so it will come back to cause delay and rework again and again. Happy Ground Hog Day!

What else can Rework cause? Rework! If the item in our example is delicate or expensive or rare, the extra handling alone may cause some damage to the part. Excess handling is anathema to former wood industry people like myself. The only thing you can do to a fine piece of wood furniture when you have to handle it and move it, is damage it. In fact, it was my Finishing Supervisor who coined the phrase I use all the time: Rework is the major cause of rework. Not only do re-worked items get handled more, since they are often treated as "bad" product they may not be handled properly, even though they still have value if we can complete the rework in a satisfactory manner. You must reinforce the concept with your employees that a rework item retains its value, but the only permanent solution is to prevent the need.

All of the above lead me to the Waste with the biggest potential: not using the combined knowledge and experience of your material handlers. The people who live with the other Wastes and the frustrations they cause have really good ideas about what they would like things to look like, how their daily work life could be more enjoyable.

Your job is to give them a voice. Teach them how to solve problems. Encourage them to try new ways of doing things. Look for the future Lean Leaders among them and give them training in leading groups of people in Continuous Improvement. Then you can really reduce and eliminate the effect of the Eight Wastes.

You must have even better examples from your own experience. I would very much like to hear them and will credit you when I use them in any future revision of this book. Let me know at alseverance13@msn.com!

Chapter Six:

Force Multiplier

Your team building effort is now beginning to pay off. You have told your people many times that they are a team. You and they have changed the way they look at their jobs and their workplace. Your team has confidence in your leadership and you are becoming a better Lean Leader. Now you can show the team how to solve the problems that frustrate them daily. Often people want to know what going Lean means to them personally. They understand that "management" wants to "cut costs", but how will those on the team benefit? After all, cutting costs in the past may have meant that there was a layoff brewing.

It is imperative to establish a policy that no one will lose their job as a result of getting Lean. The benefits gained will allow sales growth to offset any "excess" workers. And usually, the excess hours you were paying were for temporary labor and overtime anyway. Cutting these expenses saves jobs. Jobs may change as a result of solving problems and getting Lean, but no one loses their job. Instead, employees will have safer, less frustrating jobs with opportunities to grow and learn.

You must be very upfront in explaining the benefits of the Lean Initiative for each employee. Yes, the organization began this journey and asked everyone to join. Yes, the goal is to make the company more competitive by increasing quality and safely raising productivity. And there are many direct benefits for all employees. They can resolve issues that have been frustrating them. They can learn more skills. They can learn how to improve processes. They can help create their own job security, since the only job security that anyone really has is that customers continue to demand the products or services the company provides. I stress this latter point with team members every chance I have.

Using a team of employees to solve problems is a major contributor to ongoing company health and one of the best ways to eliminate the Eighth Waste.

Group problem solving done correctly will add to every team member's experience in a positive way. All will learn that they can reduce their frustrations; they will enjoy having their ideas listened to by their peers, team leaders, and supervisors; they will be the authors of successful changes.

There are many problem solving formulas available to teams. I have used a nine-step system for years that works well for complex problems or problems involving multiple departments or disciplines. I have made a practice of posting these steps in the conference room where I worked.

State the problem; identify all possible causes; identify all possible solutions; establish criteria to determine the best solution available; compare all ideas from the first three steps to the criteria, then solve the problem.

Done? No! Develop a plan to implement this solution; implement; review the results as a team. I learned this method years ago from Lee Ozley at ROI Associates and have used this successfully many times in many companies.

To achieve the best results, add the Five Whys to the second step. This is the best point in the process to drive as deeply through an issue as possible to determine the root cause of the problem. If this step is taken with proper concentration, the rest of the process becomes much simpler. Keep asking "Why?" until you have uncovered the root cause.

The Five Whys are absolutely necessary in order to have all participants think deeply and carefully about each step they propose:

What's the problem?

Production rejects 10% of the product we deliver every day.

Why?

There are too many scratches on the surface.

Why?

We have to slide the product off the stack of parts on the skid

Why?

It is too heavy to lift by one man.

Why?

One man can't reach into the pack far enough to secure the part.

Why do you do it that way?

Production has no room to accept a full skid of this part.

See what the team comes up with now, when you ask for proposals for sensible solutions. You should be getting answers that make sense for this operation, such as using a two-person lifting platform for retrieval or dropping the skid to the floor and getting help to transfer a part to the delivery vehicle. Your team will come up with ideas that make sense for your operation. Implement the team's solution and measure the results. Either the number of good products increases or it doesn't. If the number increases, is the increase large enough to offset the cost of an addition person to help handle this item? The team will find out immediately! Check the before and after U/FTE number! If you increase the cost of people by 10% and reduce handling damage to zero, you can justify the additional expense in this instance. And the actual benefit to the company is even greater than break-even! No one has to take time to deal with the scrap reporting and inventory adjustment. No one has to rework the now-damaged product or take it to the dumpster if it can't be fixed. There will eventually be a reduction in the amount of times the dumpster has to be emptied each week! And you know the cost of trash removal because you asked you accounting people when evaluating your skid recycling, remember?

Where do you get the time and talent to solve problems? You create both by changing your mindset.

Adding a person is NOT a bad thing if you use the time productively. Rather, it is an investment, no different than stopping a production line to replace a slow machine with a faster one. Do the math. If you provide 10 wazzits an hour to meet your schedule and you stop production for an hour to solve a problem, you lose 10 wazzits from today's schedule. And in our example above, when you solve the rework problem and provide 80 good wazzits every day, your company can ship 400 perfect pieces every week instead of 360, making up for the invested hour's production in just over a day's time. And you have your gain forever. Not bad – 100% shippable product AND no decrease in productivity (Units/FTE). No trade-off of quality for production!

Use your team leaders to start solving problems right away. Teach them how to facilitate a problem solving session. They must follow the formula chosen or agreed upon for everyone, so that internal customers and suppliers can be quickly integrated into even larger problem solving efforts. Use a white board to capture all ideas and answers; walk the team through the steps until a solution is proposed. Your teams are not wasting time; they are investing it in a future that will be safer, less frustrating, and more productive. And your meeting time and problem solving time will reduce as more problems are solved, more people are trained in thinking about how to solve problems, and problems get resolved on the production floor or in your warehouse in a stand-up meeting without needing a lot of conference room down time.

Everyone wins. People become the architects of their own work life and you won't have to solve every problem. This is the transition that makes Theory L work and you will lead the change from: "There's a problem but it is management's job" to find it and fix; to "Hey, boss, there's a problem." for you to fix; to "Here's a problem and I have some ideas;" to finally, "Yeah, we found a problem and we took care of it this way." That is how you know you have done your job.

Chapter Seven:

Process Improvement

Any human endeavor can be made repeatable, creating a process to do or accomplish something. We readily think of processes in manufacturing because we are making something that is visible and tangible, and it looks different after we have processed it. It doesn't matter if it is a door complete with jamb, sill, and hardware or a loaf of bread. It doesn't matter on the size of the product or the size of the operation. You can see a difference between what was delivered to a production line and what that line has done with it afterwards.

But warehousing is different, isn't it? When a warehouse material handler pulls an item from its stock location and delivers it to his customer in manufacturing, the part remains unchanged as a result. It is not different in any way at delivery than it was when first located in the warehouse. (Okay, probably dustier, but you get what I'm driving at!) In fact, you and your people probably go to great lengths to ensure that it is unchanged! There is only so much you can do to a part, and most of it is bad. You can store it, count it, and locate it. You can also scratch it, bend it, break it, or lose it! You can even keep it safe, never touch it again and still find that it's no longer usable. It can spoil, it can become obsolete, its color can fade, or it can shrink or expand in size.

So why think of process in a warehouse? Because you need to establish a correct way to locate an item so you can find it again. Because you will need to know how many you have so that shipment can be arranged when a customer wants an item that contains this part. Because your finance people want to know the value of the inventory for tax and reporting purposes. Because YOUR customer, manufacturing, wants the correct part delivered on time, in the correct quantity, and ready to use in his processes.

As a manager, you want a process in place that can be uniformly followed, easily taught to others as needed, and is universally understood. The alternative is that you will have to personally monitor and approve every move made by every material handler which is usually physically impossible and as far from Theory L as you can get. Your people want to do a good job; knowing how to do it secures them in the process.

For every operation, and for every type of part, have your workers and teams create a standardized process that becomes the job description for the operator and inventory tracker for planning and accounting. Make sure the operators own the process by having them create it, document it, and maintain it. Post it at the pull sites. Give a copy to each person who handles the product. Explain each step and use your listening skills to ensure understanding. Check with each employee periodically to confirm that they are following the process.

Here's an example of how one might look:

Process for pulling material to the production line

Summary: Safely pull only the requested amount of product in the required sequence and deliver it ready-to-use to your customer's in-bound Kanban in a timely manner, damage free.

1. Obtain the Pull List from the warehouse supervisor.

2. Proceed to the location for the oldest stock of the first part number and pick only the quantity requested.

3. Proceed to the locations of the oldest stock of each of the successive parts on your Pull List and pick only the specified quantity of each one.

4. Pull the parts in the sequence listed on your Pull List.

5. Remove and recycle all excess packaging not required for safe delivery to your customer.

6. Deliver the required product to your customer's in-bound Kanban. Remove as much additional packaging as possible and take it to the Recycling area.

7. Prior to returning for your next Pull List, check to see if any trash or rejected materials need to be removed from the production line and carry them to the designated areas.

Well, you say, what does an employee do when he or she arrives at the designated inventory location and discovers that the part number is incorrect or the quantity is wrong? What's the process then?

You need another process, obviously, and it may not involve only your warehouse people. What you create now is largely dependent on the amount of resources available to you. Some companies will want any deliverable parts brought out, even if the quantity is well short. Others will call for an immediate cycle count. Mating parts from other parts of the warehouse may have to be put back into stock.

The real response is two-fold: find a way to meet today's schedule if possible, and find a way to prevent recurrence of this or any like problems. Every interruption to the process is a signal that there is a problem to solve, and the quicker that you and your people solve these problems, the safer and more productive your jobs will be.

Think of your processes as the "current state". You have defined the way things must be done today. Now, make it your Lean tool, one that you will need to arrive at a better, future state. Discuss the existing process with your team to determine if changes need to be made. Is it safe to follow in all circumstances? Have any customers complained? Is there opportunity to improve picking times, improve delivery times, or reduce mistakes? Review any proposed changes with your customers; any benefits picked up in the warehouse could be wiped out if the change adds cost, time, manpower, or complication for them.

Process improvement may be the biggest single step you can take to tackle the Eight Wastes. The better your process, the less you will see of Over Processing and Over Production. Since Over Production can lead to Rework, you have reduced this as well. And a good process will reduce handling: the Transporting of your parts and the Moving of your people. Create good processes and hold your people accountable for following them, or you run the danger described by a prominent manufacturing executive I have worked with, who sums it up nicely: "A bad process beats a good person every time."

Chapter Eight
Quality at the Source

Tell me that you expected to see <u>this</u> topic addressed in a book about the warehouse! Of course you didn't. Quality is a production issue, after all, not a warehouse issue. Quality at the Source means that an operator will not pass a bad part or product down the production line, nor will he or she accept a bad product from the person ahead of them on that line. That's what we work so hard to teach; that is the new behavior we expect in a Lean environment. We tell our production workers that it's OK to stop the production line to fix a problem. In fact, we <u>insist</u> that they stop, though this usually requires serious re-programming of people who have been told all their working lives to "hit the number" or "make the schedule" or even to make the schedule and a little bit more. Can't hurt to get ahead, right?

For those of you asking "Why instill this idea in the warehouse?" I ask "Why not?" Every Lean manufacturing tool has a corresponding Lean warehouse tool. That's what this book is all about!

So first you will gather all your people and explain that they are expected to engage in meaningful Quality at the Source behavior. They will not deliver damaged or unusable product to their customer in manufacturing. They will not put away damaged product. They will not accept damaged or unusable product at the Receiving Dock!

One story illustrates the need for this to be understood throughout the company. At one of my clients' manufacturing plants, a subassembly area received a crate of mixed parts and of course Murphy demonstrated his presence because the parts that were needed immediately were underneath the other parts and couldn't possibly be retrieved without emptying the entire contents of the container. The team emptied the crate as quickly as they could but the interruption was long enough to briefly shut down the final assembly line for a time.

The subassembly team had reacted swiftly. They worked as quickly and diligently as possible to fix the problem, and they did the wrong thing: they reacted without any thought of their Lean training, and despite their best efforts they still shut down their customer. Luckily, the Plant Manager found this to be a teaching moment, not an opportunity to scold.

The first thing he did was discuss the issue with the warehouse supervisor who agreed that it was time in the Lean development to instruct the warehouse employees that Lean was more than just a robust 5 S effort, keeping the physical warehouse at Shine. It was time to instill Quality at the Source into the warehouse processes.

We met with every warehouse employee and described the process in detail: Safely deliver exactly what is needed to the designated in-bound Kanban in a timely manner, undamaged. This was the job, and it was not to be considered complete until their customer was satisfied. Then we told them that not only were they to deliver undamaged, usable product but that their customers were not going to accept wrong or bad product any longer! In fact, they themselves were not to put away any material that they knew to be defective, damaged, improperly packed or mixed in any kind of container.

The next meeting was with Receiving and all Receiving employees were given the same instructions: don't pass on wrong or damaged product to the warehouse to put away because they were going to bring it back!

At every step in the warehouse process, operators were to immediately begin to follow the principal of providing only good product to the next step of the process, even though this created additional work for the operators.

The benefit to production is obvious. No more incidents such as the one described above.

The benefits to the warehouse began to show themselves rather quickly, also. The first benefit was not being called to retrieve a just-delivered skid of material to be replaced and then rejected, repacked, or otherwise subjected to excess handling. The Waste of Rework was being rooted out of the warehouse. And this got easier as those putting away product ensured only good product went into the racks and storage locations.

Of course, for a time incoming material overflowed the Receiving Dock, but this, too, abated as vendors learned the hard way to supply only good product and to package it well so that it survived the trip from their plant to ours.

Not only did the bottom line immediately improve, with the reduction of scrap product and the extra time, effort, and handling that all of that entails, but every employee and supervisor knew that any subsequent scrap was internally generated. Why is this important? It tells everyone where there is a problem of process or understanding, and these problems can be fixed when they are discovered. Scrap continues to decline as proper handling, storage, and delivery improves.

A word of caution here. As you begin to eliminate bad product from your processes and warehouse you must continue in a problem-solving mode. To be truly successful in driving out bad parts, you must, as Deming said, drive out fear! You want employees to tell you that they have damaged a part. The alternative is that they hide or simply put away bad parts, a tactic that is sure to cause greater problems later.

When they approach you with the bad news, take a breath and then focus on the issue, not the person. Together, determine the cause so that you can agree on a solution. Of course it may be that employee carelessness caused the problem, but don't just assume that. Allow the employee to tell you what happened. Determine whether there is a need for equipment repair, process improvement, product placement, or additional training. Use a problem solving mode and the Five Whys to get to an agreed-upon root cause. Driving out fear will allow you and your team to build the trust necessary to keep improving.

To conclude my story, the Plant Manager in the above episode didn't stop his efforts with the completion of the warehouse retraining. He rounded up the team leaders from the subassembly areas along with every other leader whose team received material directly from the warehouse. The warehouse supervisor told them of the new processes he had installed to improve the deliveries made to the shop floor, and asked for their help and feedback during the transition. The Plant Manager made it all official. Parts in or from the warehouse were part of the plant's Quality at the Source program. If wrong or bad or damaged product was delivered to a line, it was a call to stop production and solve a problem or reinforce training. No more stopping by the customer to fix a supplier's problem or hurrying to catch up to their own customer's needs.

This Plant Manager delivered an extremely powerful message to his entire operation: we're all in this together; we all operate the same Lean way, eliminating Waste and solving problems as teams; and we will continue to look for ways to improve.

Here is another Lean quote for your collection of management aphorisms: "Lean isn't Lean if it doesn't involve everyone." – John Shook.

Chapter Nine:

Kanbans Are More Important to Warehousing Than to Production

I will begin this chapter with another definition. The word Kanban is often misused but we will use it here to mean a visible, physical location and quantity of a part. Two identical "bins" of a part needed by your customer on the production floor. The location may be in your warehouse, and I have seen this work successfully for large-scale items, but is more likely to be an area designated by production. If you think in terms of 5 S, Kanban is a logical extension of the effort your teams expend every day doing their jobs as they become Lean. Kanbans are a physical location as well as a quantity, and work best when set up in labelled in taped-off spots

Here are some more numbers for you to think about: Kanban sizes and locations. In the worst case, Kanban sizes are created by Inventory Control, using convenient history and scheduling information to decide how many PART X's are required at each production line that uses them. They don't ask for input from the production teams who use PART X and they don't ask you and your material handling teams how you deliver PART X.

Thankfully, more and more companies understand the need to have production determine the Kanban size and location. The users understand the size of the part, where it needs to be staged, how many they use in a normal shift, and how disruptive delivery of this part and subsequent removal of packaging might be.

And the best of companies do begin with the Inventory Control data, then ask the production line what it needs and asks the warehouse how it can supply PART X to the Kanban. The discussion that precedes the decision on Kanban size and location is the most important part of creating the Kanban.

Suppose we know that a quantity of 43 of PART X is needed daily and that they are too big to deliver all at once without shutting down the production line or leaving the parts so far from the point of use that each one has to be carried some distance. We know that they are received in 100 quantity lots from the vendor. Armed with this knowledge, the production team and the warehouse team can meet and determine the solution that best fits the situation. Together they will establish the Kanban size, replenishment quantity, and delivery times. They will decide where the parts will be unpackaged, who will recycle the packaging material, and how the parts are delivered.

There will be many ways to determine this Kanban replenishment. The important thing is that it is mutually agreed on by supplier and customer and is the Leanest solution they can determine. For instance, if the production line has to stop while receiving the replen, perhaps the warehouse staff can arrange to deliver at lunch or break times, taking their own break before or afterward. Or maybe there is a path that can be created and taped off that is kept free of all other supplies, people, and material so that PART X can be delivered conveniently as needed. No one knows any of these answers until the parties involved can discuss and come to a consensus on a plan.

Perhaps the initial solution is to deliver during breaks or lunch, but if this is not a good long term solution, the team deciding this must quickly work to a better answer. Maybe this only has to last a week or so until the production line can create a path, achieving a better solution. Meanwhile, the warehouse team decides it can break down the 100-piece skid and take 50 pieces in each day. While the warehouse is working on this effort, perhaps Purchasing can speak to the vendor to discuss their shipment of 50-piece lots instead of the 100-piece lots currently being received. Who knows? Maybe the vendor can supply 43 piece lots! But if you don't ask the question, you will never know!

The point of this discussion? Look back at the title I chose for this chapter. Everything decided upon will impact your team more, by definition – the goal again is to make things Lean for your warehouse and for production. You and your people have to determine how to make Kanbans work in a Lean manner for the warehouse. There are probably many things that your team can do to facilitate delivery of PART X to the Kanban as well as many ways to calculate the appropriate size of the Kanban. Keep asking questions of each other. Keep asking "Why?" five times – or more!

And resolving Kanban size for PART X is only one set of Kanbans. What will you do about all of the others that you need?

Each part or groups of parts will require some thought and planning, even if the difficulties are as not great as with PART X. Your team and your customer must consider all of the following to determine whether the selected Kanban size will last until replenishment can be made:

How many parts are needed per hour or per shift?

How large is the item?

How are the parts packaged? Can parts be unpacked prior to delivery to the floor? If so, who will do it and how will you plan for collecting the trash and recyclable packaging. If not, has the production line adequately planned for collecting the trash and recyclable packaging it will be handling? Are your material handlers responsible for trash collection? Can they immediately remove the trash and recyclables and take them directly to the appropriate drop-off points?

Will Kanban items need to be re-boxed before delivery? Is it practical to use bin size rather than count to determine Kanban size for small items such as screws?

There is one more concept I want to address and you rarely find it in the Lean literature: a "one bin Kanban." It's not addressed because Kanban means two-bin. But what do you do when it's not practical? Suppose you have a Gaylord of parts on a skid that represents some portion of the schedule for the shift. The box is delivered on the skid it came in on. The bands are cut and removed, the top opened and secured or simply cut off, and parts are easily accessible to the production workers. And there is no room for a second Gaylord; other necessary parts are located in adjacent squares. The Gaylords have to be brought in one at a time. What's the signal?

Swapping out full skids for empties can be accomplished with a radio call or Kanban light or other cue. When everyone knows the Takt time, it is easy to determine the usage cycle and plan deliveries accordingly. Sometimes you have to ignore The Book in order to do the right thing instead of doing things right; I call this simply Common Sense Manufacturing. If a one-bin "Kanban" works and makes sense for your circumstances, do it. Just keep your eyes open to the possibility of creating a two bin system if processes or layout changes to allow it. But don't agonize over "settling" when it can work perfectly well for your situation and your customer.

Chapter Ten:

Lean Inventory Control

I have focused on running a warehouse as if it were simply the supermarket that manufacturing uses to get the parts it needs, but there really is a financial need for Inventory Control. The good news is that everything you are doing to create and maintain a Lean warehouse is improving Inventory Control for the organization.

This is financially very important because a great deal of a company's cash is tied up in the inventory. Thus every improvement you make goes straight to the bottom line! You have greatly reduced the usual inventory shrinkage with your Lean approach to warehousing.

You have installed standardized processes for handling the inventory from the Receiving dock to delivery to your customer. This alone provides improved Inventory Control because you have created a culture of appropriate behaviors. Counts are conducted accurately and appropriately, before parts are put away and again when they are pulled for manufacturing. Product is treated with care and respect to reduce Waste in Waiting and Rework. Problems are reported immediately and your teams work to resolve them and prevent future recurrence. Your people prevent bad parts from being counted as good ones. They find Bill of Material errors that your engineers can fix.

Your people are trained and expected to pull the oldest product first, greatly reducing the potential for obsolescence and incompatibility with mating parts. Perfectly good items written down to zero value simply because they were forgotten, mislabeled, stored out of the way, or otherwise abandoned, are a hit to your company's bottom line that is totally unnecessary, and you and your teams have prevented these losses. Your Lean warehouse has no scrap languishing against the wall or in a dark corner. Your Lean efforts and your trained teams prevent this from happening.

Things do get broken or damaged; handling and transportation is the main cause of rework and scrap in most warehouses. Your people know that damaged items are to be reported at once, evaluated by a problem solving team and disposed of and accounted for correctly. There is no shrinkage discovered by the Physical Inventory teams because your standardized processes prevent these surprises.

At Physical Inventory, there's no clean up or prep time. Because every part is labeled, every location is accurate and labelled, because you have Sustained your 5 S Shine, the people who are conducting the inventory will find that their jobs will be merely ones of auditing your efforts. The detective work is gone! Bumps and recounts are greatly reduced or eliminated. You may have even reduced the number of locations for a given part and most certainly have fewer items with open cartons or packages in multiple locations because you have instilled the discipline of pulling the oldest product first.

You have undertaken the creation of a Lean warehouse to keep your customer happy, reduce the frustrations of your employees, and make your job easier. You have contributed greatly to the success of your business, all as you set out to do. And now the icing on the cake: cheers and accolades from your usually dour Accounting Department, because your Lean warehouse and the Lean Leaders you have found and nurtured have made even their jobs easier.

Chapter Eleven:

Lean is Forever!

This is not a trite slogan or a catch phrase. It is the most important concept for Theory L Leaders to live by. Lean is continuous improvement for your warehouse and your whole organization. There is always some additional Waste to find and eliminate. Every step you take is positive but this is a journey without an end, and you have to resolve to continue to lead this way.

Theory L is my name for the best method I know of to institutionalize Lean in an organization. Theory L leaders constantly seek ways to recruit and train others in their organization who will become Lean leaders themselves, thus insuring that the Lean initiative is sustained. For more information, please see my first book in this series, <u>The Human Side of Lean Enterprise</u>, also available from Amazon Kindle.

Your job now is to keep your Lean effort going and you must remain relentless in your message to everyone. Of course there are always new people to get up to speed. Are those you have identified as future leaders stepping up to do this? Do they take new people in hand and explain "This is how we do things around here"? Are your people understanding the integration of all the ideas you have presented? What do the behaviors show about the culture you have established?

Is your 5 S effort self-sustaining? Do your employees routinely solve problems and bring you solutions? These are the signs you have been looking for, the signs that let you know people have heard you and have become willing practitioners of Lean.

And they continue to watch you! The moment you let something slide, they will know and in a very short time everyone who works for you will know! Walk the talk. Hold everyone accountable for their behavior, including yourself!

It's ALWAYS about your people. It's your job as a leader to help your people succeed. Lead them, engage them, teach them the tools they need, and then help them succeed. In doing this, you will find the next group of Theory L Leaders from your own team.

You have created extra time in your day when you can rely on the Theory L Leaders you have identified and trained. You now have time to reflect on what you have created in your warehouse and look into the future to see what new skills will be needed as your organization grows.

My favorite author, Harry Turtledove says: "The future is here and it is coming for you." But you no longer have to worry. The future won't blindside you!

About the Author

Alan R. Severance

Senior Operations Partner
Riverton Management Consulting Group
Emmaus, PA
610-442-6373
alseverance13@msn.com

Alan Severance is a senior operations/ manufacturing executive with a successful track record of innovative and cost-effective solutions to business problems. With his strong leadership skills and experience, he has led cross-functional teams to accomplish continuous improvement of processes and product.

His experience includes leading several transformative initiatives to support market changes, integrating Sales and Operations Planning processes to ensure a consistent company-wide approach to business planning, and leading successful Lean implementations. Consequently, he is skilled in structuring organizations to effectively address current and future requirements, as well as in recruiting, training, and leading multi-disciplinary professionals to deliver high value returns on investment.

Alan's projects have helped companies improve productivity and reduce cost through his development of

Theory L Leadership, a people-centered approach to LEAN Manufacturing that emphasizes creating and empowering leaders who train others to lead. His first book, The Human Side of Lean Enterprise, is available on Amazon Kindle.

Corporate Alignment and Lean solutions are key to successful growth and continuous improvement of all organizations, not just manufacturing companies. The global economy revolves around the health of the manufacturing sectors and Alan knows and has researched methods that create a vibrant manufacturing business.

A graduate of Hamilton College, Alan earned his MBA in Organization and Management at Temple University, Philadelphia, PA.